Praise

made *of* r

"Emory's poetry is breathtakingly exquisite, a window into the heart. I found resonance, love, and beauty on every page."

— **Maggie Doyne**, author of *Between the Mountain and the Sky*

"Reading Made of Rivers *felt like coming up for air and reminded me why poetry is vital to our world. Emory Hall tenderly offers comfort and wisdom for even the most challenging experiences: love, loss, and everything in between. You can feel her heart in every piece. I will return to this collection again and again."*

— **Allie Michelle**, author of *The Rose That Blooms in the Night*

"Like sunlight pouring into your eyes when you emerge from a dark room. Emory's poems are quietly blinding. Luminous. Here, clear water meets fire. The broken heart grows big enough to contain the whole world. And praise it."

— **Mirabai Starr**, author of *Caravan of No Despair* and *Wild Mercy*

"Made of Rivers *is a love letter from the deep sea of Hall's heart to you—a necessary invitation to meet yourself where your heart is, and a testament of the magic that arises when you do."*

— **Christopher Ferreiras**, author of *The Sun Underground*

"I am blown away by the magic of Made of Rivers *and Emory Hall. Emory's words have a way of piercing right through the heart, helping us realize so much of what is felt but cannot easily be put into words. The beauty and grace with which she writes about everything from birth to grief, loss to love, is palpable. This collection will live on my nightstand for a long time."*

— **Jordan Younger**, author, podcast host, and creator of The Balanced Blonde

made *of* rivers

made of
of
rivers

EMORY HALL

HAY HOUSE

Carlsbad, California • New York City
London • Sydney • New Delhi

Published in the United Kingdom by:
Hay House UK Ltd, 1st Floor, Crawford Corner,
91-93 Baker Street, London W1U 6QQ
Tel: +44 (0)20 3927 7290; www.hayhouse.co.uk

Published in the United States of America by:
Hay House LLC, PO Box 5100, Carlsbad, CA 92018-5100
Tel: (1) 760 431 7695 or (800) 654 5126; www.hayhouse.com

Published in Australia by:
Hay House Australia Publishing Pty Ltd,
18/36 Ralph St, Alexandria NSW 2015
Tel: (61) 2 9669 4299; www.hayhouse.com.au

Published in India by:
Hay House Publishers India, Muskaan Complex,
Plot No.3, B-2, Vasant Kunj, New Delhi 110 070
Tel: (91) 11 4176 1620; www.hayhouse.co.in

Text © Emory Hall, 2024

The moral rights of the author have been asserted.

The information given in this book should not be treated as a substitute for professional medical advice; always consult a medical practitioner. Any use of information in this book is at the reader's discretion and risk. Neither the author nor the publisher can be held responsible for any loss, claim or damage arising out of the use, or misuse, of the suggestions made, the failure to take medical advice or for any material on third-party websites.

A catalogue record for this book is available from the British Library.

Previously Published by Three Rivers Publishing, ISBN: 979-8-9878-4340-6.

Tradepaper ISBN: 978-1-83782-354-3
E-book ISBN: 978-1-4019-8019-1
Audiobook ISBN: 978-1-4019-8020-7

Cover design: Christina Thiele • *Interior design:* Nick C. Welch

This product uses responsibly sourced papers and/or recycled materials. For more information, see www.hayhouse.co.uk.

Printed and bound by CPI Group (UK) Ltd, Croydon CR0 4YY

For Kai

contents

let my gardens speak for me when i am gone. let them
speak in colored whispers of all the beauty i have seen.
and felt. and lived. let them speak of how much death had
to find me; how many hard seasons it took to make me a
living, breathing thing. let them speak of my seasons of
growth and abundance, but let them also tell of my seasons
of loss and decay. let the soft, wet earth be a reminder of
hardness that didn't win. of sadness that didn't calcify.
of surrender that triumphed over resistance. and let the
glorious, fragrant blooms speak of my life and its greatest
lesson: that the beauty we make never dies.

— come sit by my garden

headwaters

water
is never broken—
this is the way
we survive.

— woman

my life is made
of rivers.
no matter how far
i trace them
across pages,
across time,
across oceans,
somehow i land
at the banks
of myself
over
and over
again.

— maps

there is an ache inside of me
that knows it won't be long
before the cool surge of an evening tide
will fill these blank pages i've been dreaming with.
the words will come, and they will carry me
to a distant shore
that i've been hunting since before i knew this calling.
what remembering it takes
to swallow up so much memory in ink.
what bravery it takes
to lay those secrets out
naked
under the light of a full moon.
the deep churning of stars turned into language.
the ancient medicine of blood and bone
distilled into story.

— writing

i was so young
but i still remember
how different
the sky looked
that day.

how even the air
felt hard
to breathe.
i can still smell
the storm,
but i cannot remember
if it was outside
or only in
my chest.

that was the day
the whole earth
shattered.
i
shattered.

it has been so long,
but sometimes i feel like
i am still picking up pieces
of myself.
still catching
my breath.

— the day you left, in august

some days
i am flooded with you.

— sister

writing
sang me lullabies
to sleep
while
my mother
grieved.

— art is a mother too

some people
will leave flowers
at your doorstep.
but i will give you
my words,
these pages,
because this
is the deepest way
i know
how to love.

— love language

spring will come
with its long light
and lessons
of how we need some seasons
of darkness
in order to bloom.
it will arrive
one morning
and drench everything
anew.

— muddied

how
the sun
brings everything inside of me
to life.

— natural

now that i am a mother
i know what my own mother lost.
now that i am a mother
i am grieving
for her.

— generations

i bloomed
out of the death
that found me.
can you still smell
the mud on me?
i reek
of resurrection.

— scars

do not dry up your gift
and scorch
the very thing
that birthed you.

— water

there is something
on fire
inside of me.

even this poetry
is baked in it.

— the calling

you came into my life
like the first whispers of spring—
all potential,
brimming with new life.
a flood of hope,
chorused with birdsong.

— a great love when it enters

the thought of being a
beginning
for someone.

not an ending,
but
a dawn.

— meeting

i long for days
with you
i never had.
sometimes
i dream
of a life
with you here.
everything looks
different.
everything looks
beautiful.

— what we lost

we are made of
a billion stories.

find someone who inhales
the scent of your pages.
who scours
word
after
word
of your epic.
who bows
at your every chapter.
who meets your end
and starts again.

— soulmate

the love that is meant for you
will always find you—
the river
always finds
the sea.

— inevitable

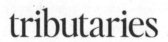

tributaries

you will break a little beneath the press of her hand on
your chest. you won't even know it's happening, for she
is quiet and works in secret. she will reach her fingers
between your bones and excavate your heart from beneath
its rib cage. she will study it, test its weight, its poverty.
she will then set it out into the wild world. there, it will
be starved and ached, but also nourished and held. all
the while, she is watching. and one day she will pull your
weathered heart back into its chest. lay it in its place and
bless it, for all that it endured and carried. she can smell
the kind of love it has now found. a love that will keep the
heart strong, blood red, alive. now, her work is done and
she must leave. for there are so many hearts still starving
to find their home. there is so much love still seeking love.
this is her hidden work.

— destiny

some people
are like earthquakes.
they break you open
and make an entirely new landscape
of your heart.

— rearranged

to think
of all the women
i had to be
to survive.
outside my window,
a burial ground
of all the faces
i have worn.
i weep for them
in secret moments—
silent eulogies
that only i will ever know.

— faces

the sounds
of a thousand foreign streets
live inside my lungs.

the colors
of a hundred different sunsets
live inside my eyes.

there are a million pieces of me
scattered
across oceans.

there are so many ways
that we never return.

— travel

creativity
is a mystical wind
that blows through my house.

sometimes sunday,
sometimes midnight.

every time it enters,
the house stays standing
and yet,
everything inside
is different.

— keep your doors unlocked

words come to me
at night
as if there is
an open doorway
to the dark heavens.
i trace sentences
like constellations
until finally
i am lost
in sleep.

dawn comes
and i can feel
their remains.
a faint echo
left on my skin.

my day is spent
searching for them.
searching for poetry
that awakes me.
that stitches my dreams
back
into dreams.
that digs up the earth
inside of me
and blooms flowers
all over
pages.

night comes
and it starts all over again.

— this is how i write

i became a river
the day you arrived.
nothing
has ever been the same.
i now stand
at the gaping mouth
without words.

— merging

i see backs bent in
prayer
plucking flowers
and planting seeds.

— the good work

even our bodies,
like sunflowers,
lean toward the sun.

we are all
aching
for light.

— longing

there are some
people
who have a wind
inside their chest.

everywhere
i go
i am
looking
for them.

— kindred

some water
will cleanse you.
some water
will drown you.
learn to spot the difference
before you dive in.

— relationships

you can be in a sea
of hurt
and a sea
of people
at the same time.

— grief

made *of* rivers

i have howled
under so many nights
trying to sound
the immeasurable
distance between our shores.

each time,
only a faint echo
of your life
returns to me.
each time,
the stars weep with me.

by sunrise,
i am left
soaked
in a dew
and a longing
that never ends.

— the distance

i laid beside you
one summer
under bent oaks,
blue sky,
and silence.

i tried to carry home
armfuls
of the grass we laid on.

but all that remained was
green stains
on my knees
and memories of you—
somewhere in the earth below.

everything i lost,
buried.

— grave

some love leaves us
with an ache so wide and deep
that we build a home
for all the pain
that lives inside of us.
our work is not
to become architects
for our houses of losses,
but rather to feel the throb of loss
so fully
that it moves through us
like water.
the hardness does not stay,
only the memory.
and what is memory but
proof
that we are
breathing,
beating
hearts.

— metabolism

it's funny how
the thing that gives me
the most words
is silence.

— writing is listening

you met death
so many times—
danced with her,
drank with her,
even knew her by first name.

and yet
you waited,
you waited,
until my son
arrived.

only then
did you leave.

— my grandfather

the way you hold on to
your light like that—
no one could ever know
all the nights
you've walked through.
what fire made you
to keep you burning like that?
tell me.

— hope is a fire

made *of* rivers

the river of that country is silent.

— the heart

time heals
let it.

the
channel

the mystery
of how we bloom
after rain,
of how we ache
with love,
of how we are made
in fire.

— growth

i have made so much beauty
from my pain
sometimes i can't tell
the difference.

— art

what will become of this story
inside my chest?

will i excavate it from my bones
give it light
and water
and air?

let it bloom into
a garden of flowers
in your name?

or will i let it stay
and let you
bury me?

this is the question
i am always asking myself:

what will become of my stories—
gardens
or
graveyards?

— the photosynthesis of healing

sometimes we must edit
the stories we tell ourselves.

— self-talk

my boundaries
are
love letters
to myself.

perhaps the most
important ones
i will ever write.

— self-love

don't fear the truth
for what it will tell you.
fear it
for what it will do
if you don't tell it.

— consumed

i have learned that
forgiveness
is a fire.
and while some fires are lit
to destroy,
others are lit
to regenerate.

i am working with the latter.
learning the heart-work
of making space
for things to bloom
where there once was
no room
for new life.

— regenerative work

i never want to be told
what it is
that i should write.
it is the only secret left
between me and god.

— autonomy

i am saying prayers
back to my body.
apologizing
for all the ways
i have cursed her.
had i known better,
i would've only ever uttered
love
into her bones.

— amends

it is by not dressing up
these words,
my stories,
that i am
most
vulnerable

but also
most
free.

— raw

made *of* rivers

i will not use language to make
certain stories
certain feelings
more beautiful
for you.
if my words make you
blush
sweat
want to run away—
this is good
this is good
this is art.

— all of me

some clarity disrupts.
find it anyway.

— truth

the sun
speaks a language
i understand.
it knows how to both rise and
fall.
it carries on,
growing things
while
burning
burning
burning.

— never apologize for the way you burn

where does your sadness point?
what direction
is it aching you toward?
what storm
is it brewing,
only to break open
the morning
of your revelation?

there is a doorway
hidden in your pain.

enter it.

— sadness as awakening

there was thunder in your voice.
you rained a million truths,
a sunshower of revelations.

your storms have a way of doing that.
of clearing things
i didn't know i needed to let go of.

— mouth

let the wilderness in.
grow a forest for a heart.
make your very blood
a salve
of pine
and open sky.
be the air
that birds come to sing in.
the water
that even rivers seek.

— wild

the secrets
the tall pines
know about me.

— forests

i was born
in a soft summer
rain.
i am most
in-season
when the sun is
high
and warm.
when the day is
long.
when the peaches
are ripe.
when the soil is
soft
and forgiving.

my body
is a house
of flowers—
i am most fragrant
in june.

— summer bones

it is such a
vulnerable
courageous
thing
to be a house for a life
and then,
after ten moons,
let them walk out
your front door

into the wild world.

— the afterbirth

ask yourself this:
does it make me softer?
if the answer is yes,
run toward it.

— ripening

you must rest.

and all at once
they fell into a deep sleep.
all the tired women
that lived inside her.

— the wound

there are oceans
waiting for you to become
a shore.

tell me,
what mountains have you built between
your heart and its own love?

— barriers

the sea

you built a life. under ten moons, you were a house of water. you held a second heart in the arms of your rib cage, dreamed two sets of dreams. merged the rivers of your bloodlines under your skin. and then, in the early hours of a spring morning, i watched a piece of you leave, swallowed in the pain of your shattering. you broke, and the rains of new life poured out of you.

you are now the mother of that dawning ground. the guardian of its soil. the mender of its aching. the gardener of its joy. this is your work now.

you were born in your dying. you were delivered to a new life as you birthed one into existence.

you are utter magic.
building that mountain.

— birth

the tides
like my breath
carry me home.

— things i learned while living by the sea

i have released
so much
into the ocean.
i swear
by now
she knows me by name.

— merging

may we find
that space of surrender
which softens
every cell.

— the cure

make peace
with all the women
you once were.

lay flowers
at their feet.

offer them incense
and honey
and forgiveness.

honor them
and give them
your silence.

listen.

bless them
and let them be.

for they are the bones
of the temple
you sit in now.

for they are
the rivers
of wisdom
leading you toward
the sea.

— i have been a thousand different women

i watch your eyes
watch the moon.
i wonder what secrets
you two are whispering about.

— unspoken

the weight of this love
is like a thousand wildflowers
sleeping on my chest.

— my son

i have abandoned
the questioning.

i have decided to let myself
make peace with uncertainty—
and *i am better for it.*
i am better for it.

— the relinquishing

lately,
i am made of softer things.
flower petals,
rain showers,
and love letters.
i have grown to adore
my tenderness.
to praise the places
where life has not hardened
but
softened me.

— soft

the way i
split open
like a fruit
and from my center
delivered
an entire forest
of dreams.

tell me
that's not magic.

— womb work

i have been
an ocean of storms.

tsunamis.
tidal waves.

and yet—
here i am.
dripping.
whole.

— the miracle

water
meeting
water.

— reflection

the way the moon moves me
i think i am an ocean.

— tidal

you left my skin so soft
after you arrived
that i was afraid my heart
might fall out of its chest.

but this is what you
continue to teach me:
that being soft
doesn't mean
i'm fragile.

there is so much strength
in the tenderness you've made.

— motherhood

i have learned
to let grief
be here.
let my body
swell,
flood,
rage,
with it.

take care of it.

let it be a
holy thing.

— acceptance

beauty is a derivative of love.

— joseph

some days,
you smell like rain.
other days,
the earth, the morning after.
i have never known anything
but to be steeped in you.

— fragrant

she asked me what it felt like—
to feel at home in my body.

"like breathing underwater
like having sunlight for bones
like an ocean for a heart
and chamomile tea for blood."

— home

there are millions of mothers
that live inside my chest.
i speak to them in quiet moments
under night skies
and in my dreams.

we are the keepers of a forest full of hearts.
the tenders of its fertile soil
the readers of its leaves
the guardians of its wild territory.

sometimes,
we dance together
drunk on the perfume of
a thousand blossoms of love.

sometimes,
we rub honey on our ribs,
broken from a thousand lifetimes
of heartbreak.

sometimes
we rest
and forget the weight we carry,
just for a moment.

i meet these mothers in secret
but they teach me everything i know.

— mothers

you came
in the soft light of dawn
as a quiet snow fell,
teaching me already
the brilliance
of letting go.

— precious jewel of snow

i've been laboring
for days
while the daffodils have
bloomed.
i haven't much to say
except that
you are the spring i've been waiting for.

— pregnant

i will make wine
from this time
and drink it
in my old age
on a rocking chair
on some porch
under a warm sun.
it will taste of
sunflowers
and books
with earthy notes
of belly laughter
and mud
and heartache.
i am already
drunk
on the memories.

— ripe

the windowsills
burst open
from lilacs peering in.
the faucets
drip honey.
the kitchen smells
of spices cooking.
there are bees
at the door.
my son
is dreaming.
it begins to rain,
softly.
my pen
spills ink
and i am taken.

— these days

if you watch your garden
closely
you will see the belly of her soil
breathe with life
and death
just like your own.

she swells
in her monsoons
just as you did
when you filled
with rainwater
and blossoms.

she exhales
in her arid seasons
and rests
for her brilliant work
of creating life
is now done.
this is how nature teaches us
to create
and
to bury
to grow
and
to let go
over and
over again.

— my body is a garden

to think
of all the poetry
that will die with us.

— unpublished

how beautifully
leaves die for us
in fall
and yet
we continue to
whisper
about death—
as if it isn't
the most
natural
thing
we do.

— cycles

time is a
devastating
beautiful
thing.

— all at once

i watch pilgrims
offer flowers
to the river.
the flowers become
the river.
the river
becomes
flowers.
they both
float away.

— impermanence

musings

musings

about the author

Emory Hall is a writer, creative, mother, and author of *Made of Rivers*. After experiencing tragic loss at a very young age, she turned to writing as a pathway to understanding her grief, and later pursued a successful career in photography. She has collaborated with her husband, musician Trevor Hall, to co-produce an EP of *Made of Rivers*. Find her at **emoryhall.com**.